YOU ARE THEM

Ratio Ethica

Copyright © 2017 Magnus Vinding

Revised edition, 2022

All rights reserved.

ISBN: 1546511504
ISBN-13: 978-1546511502

Gnothi seauton

(Know thyself)

Tat tvam asi

(That art thou)

*Please call me by my true names,
so I can wake up
and the door of my heart
could be left open,
the door of compassion.*

— Thich Nhat Hanh, *Call Me by My True Names*

CONTENTS

	Introduction	1
1	Four Reasons for Being Ethical	4
	Part I: Who Are We?	
2	Questioning Our Common-Sense View	14
3	Introducing "The Field of You"	22
4	The Realness of the Experiences of "Others"	31
	Part II: The Implications	
5	Naturalizing Value: Better and Worse States of the Field According to the Field Itself (i.e. You)	38
6	Caring About the Entire Field	44
7	The Suffering of the Field: This Is an Emergency	50
8	How Can We Reduce Suffering?	56
9	The Field View: Non Sequiturs	62
10	Realistic Paths Forward	69
	Acknowledgments	79
	Bibliography	80

INTRODUCTION

"The easiest pain to bear is someone else's"

— Unknown

Why are you the same person when you wake up in the morning as the "you" who went to sleep the night before? Why don't you instead wake up as a scared rabbit in a dark forest in the middle of the night?

Well, who says that you don't?

My claim in this book is that you in fact do. All the time. Every time a scared rabbit wakes up, that's you. In fact, this is not only true of scared rabbits the moment they wake up. It is true of all beings at all times. *You are everyone*. Or so I shall argue.

This claim seems absurd and superstitious on its face, like some feel-good New Age thinking that only a brain frying in an indecent amount of acid could entertain. Surely, I am *me*, not you.

Yet, as we shall see, it is actually our common-sense view of personal identity that is the superstitious one; and sadly, the view that I shall defend is anything but a feel-good one.

The crucial question to ask in relation to the "I am *me*, not you" sentiment stated above is: what "you"? "You" in what defensible sense? If "you" are different from me now, how are you now not different from the "you" that you claim to have been yesterday? In other words, how are spatial differences more relevant than temporal ones when it comes to what demarcates who "you" are? And are spatial and temporal differences at all relevant in the first place? I shall argue that they are not.

My argument rests chiefly upon a physicalist premise, namely that we are entirely physical beings — nothing over and above.[1] That is, there is just an evolving physical world, and sentient beings are simply different parts of this same physical world — not different soul-like entities "riding" different parts of it, as common intuition might suggest. This view is not difficult to agree with on an intellectual level, yet it nevertheless departs radically from our common-sense view of

---

[1] Support for this view can be found in Strawson, 2006.

personal identity. At the level of our intuitions and day-to-day beliefs, we are still generally lost in soul-like notions. We have yet to step beyond the grip of the evolutionarily adaptive — yet intellectually unjustifiable — ego-centric illusion of "I am me, and you are something fundamentally different", and to instead embrace a truly naturalistic view of personal identity that is consistent with what we know about the world.

This book is an attempt to take that step, in two parts. First, I will argue for such a naturalistic account of personal identity. Second, I will examine the implications of this view, particularly the ethical implications.

1. FOUR REASONS FOR BEING ETHICAL

"Reason shows me that if my happiness is desirable and a good, the equal happiness of any other person must be equally desirable."

— Henry Sidgwick, *The Methods of Ethics*

As a prelude to the following examination of personal identity, I find it worth conveying what motivates my writing this book. A helpful starting point in this regard is to look at our reasons for behaving in ethical and altruistic ways. I think we can broadly identify four such reasons.

1.1 Empathy

The first is the emotion of empathy that millions of years of evolution have hammered into us. We see someone hurting, we feel a strong empathetic impulse, and we instinctively try to help. This mechanism has enabled us to care for each other and to function together in groups, and it still seems crucial for most of what we would characterize as moral behavior today.

Yet empathy also has significant drawbacks. Being an emotion, it is subject to the biases and limits we should expect emotions to suffer from. For example, we cannot just multiply our emotions of empathy by ten when we see ten beings who are suffering. Indeed, as psychologist Paul Slovic has documented, our empathy appears to decrease as the magnitude of a disaster grows — we are generally more willing to help one victim than two victims who suffer the same ill.[2] This makes little sense from an ethical perspective.

Indeed, it is not only when it comes to numbers that our empathy betrays reason, but also when it comes to different kinds of beings. For example, most of us have significant empathy for dogs and cats, and are outraged when they are mistreated, yet when it comes to the mistreatment of equally sentient rats and pigs, tragically few of us will make any effort to object.

---

[2] Slovic, 2007.

1.2 Signaling

The power of signaling is difficult to overstate. Again, viewing ourselves in the context of our origin is instructive: we evolved in social groups, and how we were perceived in that group was critical for our survival and reproductive success. So we should expect humans to care a lot about what other people think about them, and to act accordingly.

This is arguably what we see when we observe human actions, especially when it comes to human moral behavior. Much of our do-gooding is done largely for the purpose of looking good to our peers — examples may include conspicuous donations by individuals and companies. Of course, few of us will have the self-awareness and honesty to realize and admit the prevalence of this signaling motive, yet the less than flattering truth about our motives often shines through from our actions regardless.[3]

To be sure, that we try to do good in order to look good need not be a bad thing. Indeed, it can be a great thing if we manage to exploit it efficiently. Making "alleviating the most suffering" the new "most

---
[3] Simler & Hanson, 2018, ch. 12.

championships won" or "most records sold" would no doubt constitute an enormous step of moral progress.

1.3 Consistent Reasoning

Consistent reasoning has arguably exerted a growing influence on our moral behavior in recent times. As psychologist James Flynn has documented, our ability to think in terms of consistency and other abstract concepts appears to have increased steadily since about 1930, and likely since before that. And this general pattern in cognitive development also seems to have had a significant effect on our thinking about ethics in particular.[4] Just compare how much more inconsistent we were a couple of hundred years ago compared to today in terms of allowing some arbitrarily privileged humans to own other, arbitrarily underprivileged humans. Consistent reasoning and consistency-based arguments seem to have played an important role in motivating significant changes in this regard (for example, some abolitionists appealed to notions of equal rights in their arguments against slavery).[5]

---

[4] Flynn, 2012.

Many of us now accept similar consistency-based arguments when it comes to non-human animals: we should not discriminate against sentient beings merely because they belong to a different species.[6] Humanity sadly still practices such discrimination to a staggering extent, which reveals that ethical inconsistency is by no means a thing of the past. But at least we now appear to be in a better position to begin to notice our inconsistencies, and arguments that expose our ethical inconsistencies seem to be a promising tool for inspiring further moral progress.

Consistent reasoning within the realm of ethics requires us to ask: if suffering is bad for me, why is it not equally bad for someone else? To suggest that it is not would seem inconsistent, like saying that two plus two is four for me, but it might be something else for you.

---

[5] See e.g. the 1688 Germantown Quaker Petition Against Slavery.

[6] For an elaborate case against speciesism, see Vinding, 2015; Horta, 2022.

1.4 They Are Me

The fourth and final reason for acting morally is the view that I shall argue for in this book, namely that we in a deep sense share identity with all other beings. This seems to be a relatively rare motivator for ethical behavior, at least at this point, yet this does not imply that it must necessarily remain so.

Where consistency asks us to consider *what if that were me?* the view I shall defend in this book simply amounts to the removal of the "what if" — *that really is me*. I would thus argue that the theoretical implications of this view are ultimately the same as the implications of consistent reasoning. But this does not mean that the *practical* effects of embracing them are the same. I do not think they are, and therein lies my main motivation for writing this book.

For although our conduct can be influenced by consistent reasoning to a significant extent, it seems to be a fact about the human mind that such high-minded thinking is all too easily trumped by laziness and rationalizations. Yet this seems much less true of matters pertaining to "I" — the figmental master notion in our minds that steals all attention, and which we are willing to protect at virtually any prize.

Thus, if the "I" notion in our minds becomes tied to everyone, this would, I think, make us more motivated to protect everyone than (attempts at) consistent thinking can. (I believe that has at least been the case for me.) And this, in a nutshell, is why I think this fourth reason might hold great potential when it comes to motivating us to act ethically — truly appreciating it hijacks our "me"-driven minds toward higher ethical purposes. Indeed, fully grasping it leaves no viable alternative but for us to try to improve the world.[7]

I should make clear, however, that my purpose in writing this book is not to promote ethical behavior through trickery. That is, I do not merely convey this view because I think it can help make us more ethical. I honestly see it as the truth. My goal is to make our "I"-notion correspond better with reality — with what we actually are — and I think the general claim that we are better served by having beliefs that match reality (as

---

[7] Some tentative support for the claim that this view of personal identity can help motivate moral and altruistic behavior is found in Kaufman, 2018; Diebels & Leary, 2019.

faithfully as possible) happens to be particularly true when it comes to our beliefs about personal identity.

I should also note that I do not think that this fourth and final motivation for acting ethically provides a replacement for the other motivations outlined above, but rather that it can be a strong supplement to those motivations. After all, these different motivations each serve quite distinct functions — they turn on disparate cognitive systems and styles that enable us to accomplish different things. For instance, thinking consistently about ethics may get us far and may be much needed at this point, but being a nice and socially functioning person probably also requires a good deal of empathy, along with a healthy amount of activity in cognitive circuits that are concerned with impressing our peers. In short, it seems naive to think that we can install new software in our minds that entirely supersedes, as opposed to supplements and guides, our largely signaling and emotion-driven behavior.

Indeed, I think it would be better if we were more empathetic toward those in need, if we did more to signal ethical behavior, and if we thought more in terms of ethical consistency. I have tried to promote these drivers of ethical behavior — especially thinking consistently about ethics — in my other writings. In this book, I aim to present the "they are me" view, and to in turn hopefully promote this fourth and final motivation. As physicist Freeman Dyson said of his adoption of this view: "It provided for the first time a firm foundation for ethics. It offered mankind the radical change of heart and mind that was our only hope of peace at a time of desperate danger."[8]

I have similarly high hopes about the potential impact of this view.

---

[8] Quoted in Kolak, 2004, p. xiii.

PART I: WHO ARE WE?

2. QUESTIONING OUR COMMON-SENSE VIEW

"We are a way for the cosmos to know itself."

— Carl Sagan, *Cosmos*

What do we refer to when we say "I"? The answer seems so obvious, at an intuitive level at least, that it can be hard to give an answer. If we try, however, it seems we can say that, roughly speaking, who we consider ourselves to be is the one who is born in a certain physical body — *our* body — and who then lives out a life in this body for as long as that body is alive.[9] More specifically, it seems that we largely identify the person we are with our brain, since this is where our behavioral quirks and thinking arise from. For example, most people would consider someone who has an arm amputated to be the same person, yet

---

[9] Philosopher Daniel Kolak has dubbed this common-sense view 'closed individualism', Kolak, 2004, sec 1.2.

someone who gets their brain replaced would, in the eyes of most people, be a different person.

Yet can this common-sense notion of "same brain, same person" be defended?

2.1 What We Are (Not) in Physical Terms

A problem with this common-sense view is that our entire body, including our brain, undergoes constant change throughout our lives. According to an estimate from Oak Ridge Atomic Research Center, 98 percent of the atoms that our body is made of are replaced every year, which implies that, as a matter of our constituents, we do not remain the same over time.[10]

Another suggestion has been made, however: it is not the atoms that our bodies consist of that make us the same over time — after all, they can be replaced by similar atoms — but rather the way those atoms are put together. On this view, it is the specific physical *structure* of our body, including our brain, that makes us the same over time.

---

[10] Time Magazine, 1954.

Yet this view also turns out to be problematic, since changes occur in the structure of our body and brain every second, at every level, which means that the structure of our body is not identical over time either.

However, people who refer to our structure as the defining trait of personal identity are correct in claiming that what remains *relatively* constant throughout an individual's life is the structure of their body and brain. It is plausibly this largely consistent and physically continuous structure that is the basis of our common-sense notion that different bodies are inhabited by distinct "person entities" that remain the same in each body throughout the respective lifetimes of these bodies. Yet such person-entities are, on closer inspection, difficult to reconcile with our naturalistic understanding of the world. After all, in physical terms, there is just a body that undergoes constant change while retaining a largely similar structure. There is no distinct and consistent person-entity to be found in this picture.

2.1.1 A Thought Experiment Involving Teleportation

The following thought experiment may help question our common-sense notion of personal identity. Imagine that we have invented a perfect human teleporter — a machine that can scan a body, dissolve it, and then reconstruct it elsewhere with the exact same structure. We then let this machine scan your body, dissolve it, and make it reappear in the same state right beside where your body just was. You will simply feel as if reappearing somewhere else instantaneously, and appear with the exact same structure, and hence have all the same memories, ideas, and emotions as you had just before you were dissolved.

According to the common-sense "structural" view of personal identity, this freshly assembled "you" is the same person as the one we just dissolved. After all, the state of your body would have been *more* different from your initial state if you had traveled the old-fashioned continuous way to the new spot.

Now imagine another scenario: we repeat the teleportation above, except this time we do not dissolve your original body, but let it remain so that we end up with two of "you". Yet on our common-sense view of personal identity, a person can only be one being — there can only be one "you". So the question is: which of these two resulting individuals is the same person as the original one? Which one is "you"? An intuitive response might be that you are the one who is in the same place, and not the new one, whom you, as the person who is physically continuous with the original version of you, now recognize as merely a different person with almost the same mental state as you. Yet this is inconsistent with the conclusion drawn in the first example in which "you" were teleported to a different location. At least some of the intuitions driving these conclusions need to be revised.[11]

2.2 What We Are (Not) in Experiential Terms

"… personal identity, as ordinarily understood, is presumed in, not revealed in, experience."

— Daniel Kolak, *I Am You*

Our common-sense view of personal identity can also be questioned from the vantage point of our direct

---

[11] Similar thought experiments are found in Parfit, 1984, ch. 10; Kurzweil, 2012, ch. 9.

experience. For in experiential terms, what we are is arguably an ever-changing conscious mind. There is hardly anything about our conscious experience that remains unchanged throughout our conscious lives, except, of course, for the fact that it is always conscious.[12] The self that we commonly take ourselves to be is simply a self-representation that arises in our experience. It is yet another appearance in our conscious experience, and it is therefore, in experiential terms, no more what we are than any other appearance in consciousness.

If the only thing that remains the same about our own conscious mind over time is that it is conscious, then one can reasonably argue that we, to the extent that we are the same person over time, are also other conscious beings. After all, this same fact holds equally true about them: they are also different states of consciousness, or distinct consciousness-moments, which each share the property of being conscious. In this sense, all conscious

---

[12] One could argue that, subjectively, we are not our conscious experience, but rather the witness of our conscious experience. In my view, both views are valid. In subjective terms, we are both the totality of our conscious experience (surely not any part of it more than any other, as all aspects of our experience equally are appearances *in* consciousness) and also the witness of it.

beings are fundamentally the same. Only persistent ideas and memories in our minds make it appear otherwise — as though there is something special about the mind that we call our own over time, beyond the fact that it shares more memories and has more similarities with "its own" past and future states than other minds do.

It may be objected that one's own present conscious mind does not experience the future states of other minds, and that this is the crucial difference between others and oneself. Yet while it is true that we, as a conscious mind in the present, do not directly experience the future minds of others, it is wrong to think that this constitutes a difference between other minds and the future states of what we typically consider our own mind. For the truth is that our present conscious mind does not experience the future states of "our own" mind either. The future experiences of "our own" mind will be consciousness in another state, just as much as the future experiences of what we consider other sentient beings will be consciousness in another state. Again, it is true that there is a greater similarity across the states of consciousness that we tend to regard as our own; these states will be physically continuous, and will thus tend to share more memories, thoughts, and traits altogether with our present mind than will the future minds of others. Yet that, on a physicalist view, is the *only* difference.

3. INTRODUCING "THE FIELD OF YOU"

"Every particle and every wave in the Universe is simply an excitation of a quantum field that is defined over all space and time. That remarkable assertion is at the heart of quantum field theory."

— Tom Lancaster & Stephen Blundell, *Quantum Field Theory for the Gifted Amateur*

What I have done so far has mainly been of a negative character: I have briefly rehashed a few arguments that serve to question our common-sense view of personal identity. What I have yet to do, and what I think is ultimately more interesting and fruitful, is the constructive project of outlining a positively plausible way to think about personal identity. That is what I will try to do now, by presenting a coherent view of personal identity that not only fits with what we know about the natural world, but one that, I would argue, all but immediately falls out of our modern naturalistic worldview — more specifically, of quantum field theory.

3.1 Quantum Field Theory — A Different Way of Seeing the World

Our minds tend to think in terms of objects. When we look out at the world, we perceive a myriad of fundamentally distinct objects that occupy different parts of space. This is a useful way to think about the world. It is also, ultimately, an inaccurate way to view the world, at least according to our best, most accurate theory of the physical world: quantum field theory — the theory that Richard Feynman reportedly claimed has an accuracy corresponding to being able to predict "a distance as great as the width of North America to an accuracy of one human hair's breadth."[13]

---

[13] As quoted in Joot, 2012, p. 153. What Feynman was talking about, in more concrete terms, was quantum electrodynamics, the quantum field theory of electromagnetism where relativistic effects are taken into account.

Rather than seeing the world as consisting of fundamentally distinct "things" that occupy different parts of space, quantum field theory understands any particle as an excitation of an all-pervading quantum field. One may think of this field as a fabric, and what we recognize as matter is then a certain state of vibration of this fabric, not some separate entity that is placed "in it". On this view, when you see a person running, what you see is not really a material object (the runner) that moves through a non-material medium (space), but rather a (very complex) state of excitation that is moving through an all-pervading field, like an intricate wave moving through the ocean. This is a radically different way of seeing the world.[14]

---

[14] One may ask whether quantum field theory is a true description of reality. There are certainly phenomena that we have not been able to explain in terms of quantum field theory so far, gravity being one of them (physicists are working on it). Yet quantum field theory still appears to represent our best, most thoroughly tested understanding of the natural world at this point, cf. Lancaster & Blundell, 2014, p. 1; Carroll, 2021. And I believe this — our best understanding of the natural world — should ideally form the basis of our view of personal identity, cf. Flanagan, 2003; Pearce, 2014.

3.1.1 One Field or Many?

According to quantum field theory, different kinds of particles can be described as excitations of different quantum fields. This is not, however, to say that they cannot be described in terms of a single underlying field — some physicists are searching for a unified field theory that does exactly that. We do not yet know whether such a unified field theory exists, yet whether it does is not critical in this context. For whether the world is comprised of a set of all-pervading fields, or whether it is comprised of a single such field that we presently describe in terms of many fields, the end conclusion is the same: everything we observe, from photons to blue whales, are excitations of the same all-pervading "fabric" — the set of the all-pervading field(s) that quantum field theory describes. For the sake of simplicity, I shall from now on simply refer to this fabric as 'the Field' with a capital F.

3.2 The Implications for Personal Identity

Taking this view of the world seriously not only undermines our common-sense view of personal identity, but also forces us to replace it with a new, rather specific one. Where we used to think of different persons as being in some sense different objects that emerge and disappear over time, the above-mentioned view of the world implies that the entire world is comprised of the same all-pervading "object". And the vibrations of this object in different times and places comprise everything we see in the world, including what we consider to be different persons. Crudely put, the world is comprised of an all-pervading "substance" that takes on a myriad structures; it is not a structure that contains a myriad distinct substances.

This may all seem quite abstract, so perhaps it is worth considering the concrete case of birth and death. On our common-sense view, when a person is born, a new object (and subject) has in some sense emerged, and when this person dies, this same object disappears. We have a fairly binary view: we go from zero to one (birth) and eventually back to zero again (death).

On the Field view, however, there are no objects emerging or disappearing. There is just the Field that in some places jiggles itself into the form of a body with a sentient mind as we know it — what some will

recognize as a highly complex biological process —
and it then eventually jiggles itself out of this form. The
Field remains. It merely underwent structural change,
not substantive change, and it will keep on doing so.
This is true over time and space, both about (what we
commonly consider) other persons and ourselves: only
the structure is different, the fundamental substance is
the same.

3.2.1 No *In*carnation

One might think that the view described above entails
reincarnation. Yet this is not the case. Indeed, the Field
view, along with any other physicalist view, is in some
sense the very antithesis of any "reincarnationist" view.
The reason being, in short, that belief in reincarnation
still amounts to a dualist view.

Most people, whether they believe in reincarnation or
not, appear to embrace an intuitive dualism. We
generally do not view ourselves *as* a physical body, but
rather as someone who is in some sense in possession
of a body, as a non-physical agent who is riding the
body like a vehicle. And we generally see other beings

in the same way. We see sentient beings as *placed in* a certain part of the physical world, not *as* (a certain part of) the physical world.

Reincarnation is dualist in the sense that it rests on the above-mentioned vehicle view of sentient beings, and where it departs from Western "common-sense" dualism is simply in its claim that the same "driver" is going to jump from vehicle to vehicle over time, like a clothespin that jumps from one piece of fabric to another. This is not compatible with the Field view expressed above. On this view, there are no clothespins. Only the fabric exists, and what we recognize as a conscious mind *is* the fabric itself, vibrating in certain complex states.

Yet it is important to note, again, that even those of us who do not believe in reincarnation still tend to buy into the clothespin view of sentient minds.[15] The only difference is that we do not think that the clothespin jumps around. Rather, our view seems more akin to the

---

[15] Even the common and apparently humble claim that "we simply do not know what happens to us when we die" secretly contains this premise that there is a "we" that is somehow different from the body, as opposed to the "us" simply *being* the physical, in which case there is no mystery. What happens to "us" is what happens to the Field.

belief that the clothespin simply dissolves as the body it rides around in dies — that something disappears, as opposed to merely changing state.[16]

Put simply, on the Field view, there is no "you entity" jumping around or disappearing. There is only the Field changing state, and some of these states are evidently sentient. What we consider different beings is ultimately this same Field in different states.

---

[16] Erwin Schrödinger made a similar point in his conclusion of *What Is Life*:

> Are we not inclining to much greater nonsense, if in discarding their gross superstitions we retain their naive idea of plurality of souls, but 'remedy' it by declaring the souls to be perishable, to be annihilated with the respective bodies? The only possible alternative is simply to keep to the immediate experience that consciousness is a singular of which the plural is unknown; that there is only one thing and that what seems to be a plurality is merely a series of different personality aspects of this one thing, produced by a deception (the Indian MAJA); the same illusion is produced in a gallery of mirrors, and in the same way Gaurisankar and Mt Everest turned out to be the same peak seen from different valleys. There are, of course, elaborate ghost-stories fixed in our minds to hamper our acceptance of such simple recognition.

In more concrete terms: my deceased grandfather was a pattern of the Field. There was no "him" apart from the Field that emerged or disappeared. The Field just changed, and now it has a different state that includes the mind-brains that we call "your mind" and "my mind". Across time and space, we are the same "object" vibrating in different ways. And this, I submit, is the only naturalistically sound way of thinking about yourself, namely *as* this Field — "the Field of You".

4. THE REALNESS OF THE EXPERIENCES OF "OTHERS"

"Others' consciousness is the best kept secret in the universe, masquerading in the form of physical gestures and sounds."

— Jonathan Leighton, *The Battle for Compassion: Ethics in an Apathetic Universe*

An obvious yet significant point is the fact that the experiences of those parts of the Field that we consider "other individuals" are real. *Truly, really **real**.* This is trivial to say, of course, and nobody would disagree. Yet to really appreciate it is, I think, anything but trivial. As philosopher David Pearce has noted, we tend to see others as objects with feelings, rather than as fellow subjects of experience.[17] And this, I believe, is among the main reasons we are deluded about personal identity.

---

[17] Personal communication.

We know that the experience that resides in the place we call "our own head" is real. We know that it is real now and that it will be real tomorrow. However, when it comes to the experiences of those we consider other sentient minds, this fact is somehow much less salient.

Our appreciation of the reality of others' experiences is somewhat analogous to our knowledge that there is magma some thousands of meters beneath our feet. Any educated person knows this, yet this knowledge still remains a lot less vivid than, say, our knowledge of what the Earth is like on its surface. We are reminded of the latter every day, while the former is only apparent to us upon a bit of recalling and reflecting on what we have been told. And yet, even upon reflection, we probably still only have a rather weak grasp of the fact that some number of kilometers beneath us, there *really* is an ocean of melted rocks. We quickly forget all about it and return our gaze to the more relevant and interesting surface environment in which we find ourselves.

The experience that resides in what we call "our own head" is much like the surface of the Earth: we are reminded of its realness every day. We continually feel and taste its reality, as well as remember it, and thus we can easily project its reality into the future. The minds of "others", in contrast, are more akin to the tons of magma beneath us — sure, none of us would deny that they exist, yet to *really* appreciate and connect with their realness can be difficult and may feel like a needless distraction for our minds. After all, our Darwinian minds mumble, what is the point of all this 'really appreciating'?

4.1 "I'm Special" — A Predictable Belief of a Darwinian Mind

Such mumbling is not surprising. Our minds are not optimized for finding the truth. Rather, our ability to uncover truths ultimately evolved because it was useful for our survival and reproduction. And when the truth is in conflict with surviving and reproducing in an environment ruled by natural selection, the truth generally loses.

This might help explain why it can feel inconvenient to acknowledge that the experiences of those parts of the Field that we consider "other sentient minds" are just as real as the narrow thread of experiences that we consider our own. Keeping this truth clearly in view is unlikely to be a recipe for gene propagation. Stubbornly ignoring it seems a much better strategy, as it enables us to be bigoted with abandon, and to concentrate all our focus toward the body that we consider our own — the vehicle of our genes. It allows us to turn the suffering of distant others into mere abstractions that carry virtually no motivating force.

4.2 Making Reality Fit Preconceived Intuitions

Our preconceived intuitions are so powerful that even the philosophy of personal identity has often consisted in the question-begging effort of trying to make common-sense notions of personal identity fit with reality, as opposed to questioning the sensibility of our common-sense intuitions in the first place.[18] This has

---

[18] As philosopher James Giles put it (Giles, 1993): "The problem of personal identity is often said to be one of accounting for what it is that gives persons their identity over time. However, once the problem has been construed in these terms, it is plain that too much has already been assumed."

resulted in attempts to answer questions such as:

"What makes you a different person from me?"

"What makes me the same person over time?"

"If we gradually replace your neurons one at a time, when will your brain no longer be 'you'?"

These questions arguably only make sense within our preconceived framework of personal identity. From the perspective of the Field view, those questions can be answered, or perhaps rather dissolved, as follows:

"What makes you a different person from me?"

What we call "you" and "me" are different states of the same Field.

"What makes me the same person over time?"

There are no clothespins that make us the same person over time in a sense that renders us different from others. There is just the Field continually changing state, and all consciousness-moments are different parts of this same Field.

"If we gradually replaced your neurons one at a time, when would your brain no longer be 'you'?"

The Field would merely undergo change. The essentialist "you" invoked in this question was never there in the first place, whereas you, as the Field, remain.

In sum, we are not what our Darwinian intuitions tell us we are. What we are is the Field in different states of vibration. Or in phenomenological terms: we are consciousness in different states, all of which are equally real, equally experienced by the Field. And, as I will argue in the second part of the book, we would be better off trying to make our view conform to reality rather than trying to go the other way around.

Part II: The Implications

5. NATURALIZING VALUE: BETTER AND WORSE STATES OF THE FIELD ACCORDING TO THE FIELD ITSELF (I.E. YOU)

"Value, and conversely disvalue, are distinctive features literally inherent in the world no less than phenomenal redness; and thus there can be objective, truth-evaluable judgements of value. This property is mind-dependent, hence brain-dependent, hence a natural and objective property of the world."

— David Pearce, *The Hedonistic Imperative*

Upon embracing a physicalist view, it seems that ethics must relate to the particular states that the physical world can assume, as there is then ultimately nothing else that ethics *can* be about. I will argue that this is indeed what ethics is all about: optimizing the Field that we are so as to prevent the worst states from being realized and to bring better ones about instead.

This is in some sense already what we try to do most of the time, although only locally and inefficiently. For example, we listen to music and consume entertainment because it brings us in a better state and helps us avoid bad states. It is a local optimization effort. The grand ethical task before us, I submit, is to expand this effort into an all-inclusive one, so that we optimize the *entire* Field that we are rather than a tiny subset — an expansion that follows naturally from realizing our own identity *as* the Field.

5.1 "That's Merely What You Want"

One might object that there is no such thing as universal ethics — there are just different individuals who want different things, and these individuals sometimes confuse their wants for some sort of "universal" or "objective" ethic. Thus, belief in the existence of universal ethics of any kind is just the predictable product of confused social primate minds that project their own moral intuitions onto the world at large.

I think this objection gets a number of things wrong, which I think are worth exploring. First, as a preliminary note, it is worth highlighting that the universal view of ethics laid out above is among the last things that one would expect to be an intuitive suggestion from a human mind. Indeed, what one would expect our human intuitions to endorse is roughly the opposite, namely that we should just care about ourselves in the narrowest sense, along with those who share our genes.

Second, I believe the objection above smuggles in dualism, in that it rests on a covert separation of "you" and "the natural world", as though sentient minds were not part of the natural world. But sentient minds *are* part of the natural world. In particular, a sentient mind that finds its own state painful and worth avoiding *is* a local part of the Field that finds its own state painful and worth avoiding — not something separate from the Field. Being in such a state is, I submit, inherently disvaluable, and that disvalue is ultimately a property *of the Field*.

Specifically, if you take my mind-brain in a state of extreme pain that I want to stop, and instantiate it anywhere in the Field, the Field will, at this particular locality, be in a state of extreme pain and will want it to stop. It is a universal property of the Field that that particular brain state will feel bad and unwanted no matter where in the Field it is instantiated. It is not, of course, that there is some kind of dormant will in the Field that quietly wants to avoid certain states, but just that certain states of the Field are inherently painful and worth avoiding, according to the Field itself. And this is not a matter of choice; after all, when we are in a state of extreme suffering, we cannot simply choose to consider it benign or decide not to care about it.

Put briefly, bad states of sentience are not something that exist over and above the states of the Field itself, and they are not bad and worth avoiding according to some clothespin over and above physical reality. They are bad *according to the Field itself when in that state.* Indeed, there is nothing else that could declare the badness of these states than the Field itself.

5.2 "What About Conflicts Between Different Parts of the Field?"

What about cases where the need for relief in one part of the Field is in conflict with that of another part? How can we measure different states of need and disvalue against each other?

First, it is worth noting that ethics (i.e. Field optimization) need not be all about conflict. We are very inclined toward zero-sum thinking, yet there is no reason to think that Field optimization must be a zero-sum game in the sense that the gain in one part of the Field must happen at an equal cost elsewhere.

That being said, it must be acknowledged that this question about the relative priority of different needs and interests is a difficult one. What we *can* say, however, is that we can make at least *some* confident judgments about which states that are worse and more worth preventing than others. For instance, it is clear that, other things being equal, a state of extreme suffering is worse than an ordinary headache, and such a headache is in turn worse than an untroubled state.

One may object to these general evaluations because they do not take account of *whose* suffering we are talking about. Yet this objection makes little sense in light of the Field view. Upon adopting this view, there is ultimately no reason to consider one state of suffering more worthy of priority than an equal state of suffering found elsewhere, since it all occurs in the same Field.

In sum, I maintain that the Field that we are can assume truly better and worse states. Specifically, states such as extreme suffering are universally worth avoiding according to the Field itself — *ourself*. And I believe that acknowledging this universal truth is crucial in order for us to start systematically optimizing the Field, by moving ourself away from states of extreme suffering and toward better states. This endeavor is worth pursuing, according to ourself, for no one's sake but our own.

6. CARING ABOUT THE ENTIRE FIELD

"The question is not *Can they reason?* or *Can they talk?* but *Can they suffer?*"

— Jeremy Bentham, *The Principles of Morals and Legislation*

An obvious implication of the Field view is that we should care about the *entire* Field, at least all those states of the Field that are sentient. Yet while this claim may be easy to agree with in the abstract, it can nevertheless be difficult to fully internalize it. Our moral sentiments are built by a complex interplay of genetic and cultural factors, and a nod of agreement to the principle of "concern for all", however sincere, does not recalibrate these sentiments right away. It is at best the first step toward such recalibration.

When it comes to caring about the entire Field, there is one bias that is particularly strong, namely our speciesist bias.[19] In this day and age, "caring about everyone" is virtually synonymous with "caring about every human individual", which is why merely saying that we should "care about everyone" is insufficient on its own. We need another cognitive tool in order to prevail against our bias. We need, I will argue, to think in terms of anti-speciesism.

6.1 Anti-Speciesism

If we grant that sentience is ultimately what matters — or at least that it is a crucial *part* of what matters — it seems that we cannot justify our discrimination against sentient beings based on their species membership. Just as an individual's race, sex, or sexual orientation is ethically irrelevant, it is not morally relevant which species a sentient being belongs to.[20]

An objection might be that human individuals are more sentient than individuals of other species, and hence our greater concern for humans is generally warranted. Yet this objection is problematic for a number of reasons.

---

[19] Caviola et al., 2019.

[20] See also Horta, 2022.

First, even if non-human beings were less sentient than human beings, this would still not imply that our severe discrimination against them is justified. After all, if a given human individual were somehow shown to be less sentient than another, we would not find it acceptable to give significantly less moral consideration to the former, let alone disregard the less sentient individual completely (e.g. accept that we can exploit and kill that individual).

Second, the claim that humans are more sentient than other sentient beings — e.g. that humans experience pain more intensely than other beings — is arguably not supported by the evidence. As David Pearce notes:

> We often find it convenient to act as though the capacity to suffer were somehow inseparably bound up with linguistic ability or ratiocinative prowess. Yet there is absolutely no evidence that this is the case, and a great deal that it isn't. The functional regions of the brain which subserve physical agony, the "pain centres", and the mainly limbic substrates of emotion, appear in phylogenetic terms to be remarkably constant in the vertebrate line. The neural

pathways involving serotonin, the periaquaductal grey matter, bradykinin, dynorphin, ATP receptors, the major opioid families, substance P etc all existed long before hominids walked the earth. Not merely is the biochemistry of suffering disturbingly similar where not effectively type-identical across a wide spectrum of vertebrate (and even some invertebrate) species. It is at least possible that members of any species whose members have more pain cells exhibiting greater synaptic density than humans sometimes suffer more atrociously than we do, whatever their notional "intelligence".[21]

The possibility that beings of other species may even experience suffering *more* intensely than humans has been raised by others as well, including zoologist James Serpell who notes that, unlike other animals, humans can rationalize their pain, which to some extent helps to rationalize it away.[22] Richard Dawkins has likewise argued for the plausibility of this claim:

---

[21] Pearce, 1995, sec. 1.9. See also Low et al., 2012.

[22] See about ten minutes into the movie *Speciesism: The Movie*.

> ... I can see a Darwinian reason why there might even be a negative correlation between intellect and susceptibility to pain. ...
>
> Isn't it plausible that a clever species such as our own might need less pain, precisely because we are capable of intelligently working out what is good for us, and what damaging events we should avoid? Isn't it plausible that an unintelligent species might need a massive wallop of pain, to drive home a lesson that we can learn with less powerful inducement?
>
> At very least, I conclude that we have no general reason to think that non-human animals feel pain less acutely than we do, and we should in any case give them the benefit of the doubt.[23]

Add to these considerations that non-human beings constitute the vast majority of sentient beings on the planet — more than 99.99 percent of vertebrates are non-human, and that is only counting vertebrates[24] —

---

[23] Dawkins, 2011.

[24] Tomasik, 2009.

and it becomes apparent just how skewed and unjustified our prevailing ethical focus is. Almost all of our moral attention is devoted to much less than 0.01 percent of the sentient beings within our reach.

Again, this remains true for most of us even when we accept that we should care about the entire Field. Our moral sentiments do not immediately catch up with our intellectual insights, if they ever fully do, which is why it is helpful to supplement the general ideal of caring about the entire Field with the more specific ideal of anti-speciesism.[25]

---

[25] For a fuller case against speciesism, see Vinding, 2015; Horta, 2022.

7. THE SUFFERING OF THE FIELD: THIS IS AN EMERGENCY

"It's easy to convince oneself that things can't really be that bad, that the horror invoked is being overblown, that what is going on elsewhere in space-time is somehow less real than this here-and-now, or that the good in the world somehow offsets the bad. Yet however vividly one thinks one can imagine what agony, torture or suicidal despair must be like, the reality is inconceivably worse. Hazy images of Orwell's 'Room 101' barely hint at what I'm talking about. The force of 'inconceivably' is itself largely inconceivable here."

— David Pearce, *The Hedonistic Imperative*

The idea that extreme suffering has moral priority above anything else seems hard to deny, at least when we are confronted with it directly, either by seeing others endure such suffering or by experiencing it ourselves. Extreme suffering begs for urgent action.[26]

If we are suffering intensely, we do not hesitate to do something about it, and all talk about ethics seems overly theoretical and unnecessary. The reality, however, is that we *are*, as the Field, enduring such suffering all the time, and at an enormous scale. Yet due to ignorance and normalization of this suffering, we fail to act.

7.1 The Normalization of Disaster

In 1755, an earthquake occurred southwest of the coast of Portugal, the so-called Great Lisbon Earthquake, which led to a tsunami estimated to have killed 12,000 to 50,000 people in Lisbon alone. This tragedy made a great impression on many of the philosophers of the time due to its magnitude and conspicuous lack of meaning. For how, they had to wonder, can there be a good God in a world where such an enormous and utterly meaningless tragedy occurs? It seemed too much

---

[26] For more elaborate arguments for the ethical primacy of suffering, see Mayerfeld, 1999; Tomasik, 2016; Vinding, 2020, Part I.

of a stretch, as Voltaire tried to express in his satirical novella *Candide,* published four years after the tragedy.

This reaction makes a lot of sense when we think about the psychological effects of such a tragedy. Our brains process the news of such disasters with strong emotions, which is unsurprising given our evolutionary history: paying serious attention to an enormous disaster that affects us or our kin is exactly what we should expect an organism like ourselves to do.

Yet the reaction makes less sense when we look at the actual scale of suffering in the world. For the truth is that, in terms of suffering endured, a disaster on a far greater scale than the Great Lisbon Earthquake takes place every single day on Earth — every single minute even. It is just less concentrated in space, and less unusual.

For example, even in the 1750s Europe, not just thousands but millions of people died every year in ways that were hardly much less painful than the deaths caused by the Lisbon Earthquake. Should these deaths and the suffering involved be considered less bad just because they were more distributed over space and time than those that occurred in Lisbon? That seems difficult to defend. Yet the dispersion and normality of this suffering made it harder for the philosophers of the time to notice it in the same way — to *feel* a sense of horror remotely proportional to the scale of the disaster.

Of course, the deeper point here is not about philosophers of the past, but rather about all of us today, and how we are out of touch with the facts of the condition in which we are living. Suffering on an enormous scale is not, unfortunately, a thing of the past. It is real today, right now, on a massive scale that far surpasses any of the tragedies described above, and yet we fail to realize it just the same.

For not only do millions of people still suffer and die every year — with more than a million of these deaths being due to readily preventable causes — but humanity now exploits, mistreats, and kills more sentient beings than ever before in history. Tens of billions of non-human beings are tormented and killed every year at human hands, yet most of us fail to *feel* the urgency of this moral catastrophe, because it is so normalized. As George Bernard Shaw observed:

"Custom will reconcile people to any atrocity".[27]

Yet the incomprehensibly bad horror story that is humanity's mistreatment of other sentient beings still only constitutes a small fraction of all the horror that takes place on our planet, as the number of beings who suffer and die in nature is orders of magnitude greater than the number of beings humanity exploits and kills.[28] In nature, innumerable non-human beings suffer and die due to starvation, disease, and being eaten alive, among other causes; and just like humans, these beings have an interest in not enduring such suffering. In terms of the scale of suffering, this is by far the biggest disaster on the planet. And we are barely even talking about it.[29]

This is the world we are living in. Or rather, this is the state of the Field that we *are*. Every day, a catastrophe on a scale far greater than those reported in any history book is taking place. And we feel next to nothing about it. On both an emotional and intellectual level, we are deeply out of touch with reality.

---

[27] He wrote this in the preface of *Killing for Sport* (1915), edited by Henry Stephens Salt.

[28] Tomasik, 2009.

[29] Pearce, 2012; Tomasik, 2015a.

The ongoing catastrophe that is taking place around us is all baseline horror, and hence we fail to recognize it as such, and to acknowledge the ever-present urgency of doing something about it. Most of us realize that if we had found ourselves in Germany in the 1930s, it would have been urgent for us to do something to prevent future horrors. Yet the truth is that we are in roughly the same position today. We are in as good a position as ever to save countless individuals from pain and suffering.

Once we realize our identity as the Field, and once we acknowledge the true horror of extreme suffering, the primacy of reducing suffering throughout the Field becomes self-evident, inescapable even. For if you are getting eaten alive, boiled alive, or suffer a similarly horrible fate — and you are, in a frightfully real sense — the implications are clear. You do not ignore or rationalize the suffering. You urgently do your best to alleviate it.[30]

---

[30] Of course, a universal view of personal identity is by no means required to reach this practical conclusion. One can reasonably argue that basic compassion alone implies massive efforts to prevent extreme suffering.

8. HOW CAN WE REDUCE SUFFERING?

"We have enormous opportunity to reduce suffering on behalf of sentient creatures."

— Brian Tomasik, 'Against Wishful Thinking'

How can we alleviate and prevent suffering in the world? While it is far from clear how to best reduce suffering, and while there will always be uncertainty about the consequences of our actions, there are still many things we can do today that are likely to be highly beneficial.

8.1 Raising Concern for Suffering and Expanding Our Moral Circle

A promising strategy we can pursue is to raise concern for suffering so that we make its reduction a priority. If we make reducing suffering on behalf of all sentient beings a clear and widely shared goal, it seems much more likely that we will be successful in achieving this goal, both today and in the future.[31]

How to best raise concern for suffering is an open question, yet it seems that a combination of arguments and direct exposure to the realities of suffering, in the form of pictures and vivid descriptions, can be quite effective.[32] As for how we can expand our moral circle, a similar strategy of presenting arguments and exposing ongoing cruelty and suffering endured by non-human beings seems promising.[33]

8.2 Advancing the Universal View of Personal Identity

As noted in the introduction, I believe that the view of personal identity I have argued for here may hold great potential as well, in combination with the strategies

---

[31] Tomasik, 2015b; Vinding, 2020, ch. 12.

[32] See e.g. Mayerfeld, 1999; Tomasik, 2013c; 2016; Vinding, 2020.

[33] See e.g. *Speciesism: The Movie* by Mark Devries, as well as Vinding, 2015; Horta, 2022.

listed above. Indeed, on the all-encompassing view of personal identity, even psychopaths may become dedicated toward helping apparent others. For as one study found, it is not that psychopaths cannot care at all. Rather, it seems that they just do not care about those whom their minds identify as "others":

> Our results demonstrate that while individuals with psychopathy exhibited a strong response in pain-affective brain regions when taking an imagine-self perspective, they failed to recruit the neural circuits that were activated in controls during an imagine-other perspective, and that may contribute to lack of empathic concern.[34]

So if psychopaths imagine what they see happening to others as occurring to themselves, it seems that they *do* feel and care, which tentatively suggests that a more expansive view of personal identity could make them more prosocial, or at least that it could help discourage acts of cruelty.

---

[34] Decety et al., 2013.

Yet it is not only psychopaths who might become more ethical upon adopting such a view. After all, most of us tend to have rather ego-driven minds, ruled mostly by a motivation to "make the future better for myself", which suggests that construing this notion of "myself" as the entire Field could help make us more motivated to make the future better for all its sentient states.[35]

8.3 Researching and Reflecting on the Question

There are many open questions before us when it comes to how we can best alleviate and prevent suffering, which suggests that we should make research on such questions a priority. These include questions such as: How do we best raise concern for suffering? How do we best expand our circle of moral consideration? And how can we avoid the greatest risks of the worst kinds of suffering?

---

[35] Again, tentative support for the claim that this view of personal identity can help motivate moral and altruistic behavior is found in Kaufman, 2018; Diebels & Leary, 2019.

Better answers to these questions would be of great value, and it seems that the only way we can hope to approach such answers is through further research. Although our sense of urgency is more tied to direct action than to doing research on crucial questions, the latter is indeed an urgent necessity as well. The more we know, the more qualified we are to create a better world.[36]

8.4 Donating to the Cause

There are many ways to donate to the cause of alleviating and preventing suffering in the world. Dedicating one's time to one or more of the pursuits outlined above, professionally or otherwise, is one way. Another way is to donate money to the cause, such as by donating to organizations that do effective activism or research. Some organizations that work on reducing suffering on behalf of all sentient beings include Animal Ethics and the Organisation for the Prevention of Intense Suffering (OPIS).

---

[36] For more on the importance of research, see Vinding, 2020, ch. 16; Vinding, 2022b.

In sum, there are many ways in which we can dedicate our time and resources toward the effective alleviation and prevention of extreme suffering.[37]

---

[37] For a deeper examination of how we can best reduce suffering, see Vinding, 2020; 2022a.

9. THE FIELD VIEW: NON SEQUITURS

In this chapter I shall address some non sequiturs — i.e. apparent yet fallacious implications — that one may be tempted to draw from the Field view of personal identity and ethics that I have defended here.

9.1 Narrow Self-Care

The first non sequitur is that the Field view would imply that one should not put a high priority on taking good care of oneself, in the usual narrow sense. But in order to alleviate suffering in effective ways, one must have good mental and physical health, which in turn requires quality self-care and self-investment. The choice between a life where one takes good care of oneself — a life with good relationships, healthy self-respect, personal growth, financial security, etc. — or a life where one works to alleviate suffering is a false one, quite fortunately. The former is necessary if the latter is to be possible in a sustainable way. We have good reasons to take good care of ourselves, and embracing the Field view gives us more such reasons.[38]

9.2 The Sensibility of Distinctions and Respect for "Others"

Even if we all share personal identity in a deep sense, it is still true that, in another sense, we do not. And distinctions and differences between different individuals clearly matter. Yet this is not contrary to the Field view. After all, the Field view in no way implies that we cannot meaningfully distinguish between others and ourselves in the ordinary sense, any more than it implies that we cannot distinguish between, say, ourselves at age 18 and 25. What the Field view implies is just that distinctions like these — such as that between (what we usually consider) two different persons and between ourselves at different ages — are far more similar than our clothespin intuitions will admit, in that neither of them are distinctions between fundamentally different "things".

---

[38] More on healthy and sustainable self-care aimed at a higher compassionate purpose can be found in Vinding, forthcoming.

That being said, there are indeed relevant differences between these two kinds of distinctions. Michael on Monday clearly stands in a different relation to Michael on Tuesday than he does to others. He knows far more about the experiences and preferences of Michael on Tuesday than does anyone else, and he probably has a better sense of how he can help himself and others than does virtually anybody else. It thus makes sense that he can make decisions on behalf of his future self in ways that he cannot on behalf of others.

In general, the importance of personal autonomy is by no means diminished by the Field view, since we still have an interest in being free from unwanted infringements, and since a lack of personal autonomy and liberty likely would have very bad consequences overall.[39]

---

[39] Vinding, 2022a, ch. 11.

9.3 The Importance of Thinking About Ethics in Different and Nuanced Ways

The necessity of respect for personal autonomy ties into a broader point, which is the importance of thinking about ethics in a multitude of ways. Thinking about ethics in terms of Field optimization can, I think, be a valuable addition to our toolbox of moral reasoning, but, as argued in the discussion about anti-speciesism, it is far from sufficient on its own. We also need to emphasize the importance of virtues, strict rules, and prosocial feelings, all of which serve important roles in the reduction of suffering.[40]

Similarly, upon embracing a universal view of personal identity and ethics, it may be tempting to conclude that we should not have deeper emotional connections with some beings than we do with others. Yet this is a non sequitur, not least because deep emotional connections with those closest to us tends to be indispensable for our ability to function and to contribute in the world.

---

[40] Ajantaival, 2021a.

9.4 Death and the Hereafter

Finally, it is worth clarifying what the Field view of personal identity implies — and what it does not imply — about death and "the afterlife", since this is another set of subjects where it is tempting to draw simplistic and misguided conclusions.

As mentioned already, the Field view does not imply reincarnationist views in any traditional sense, but is rather the very anti-thesis of such views. Yet that is not to say that all notions of an afterlife are incompatible with the Field view. Indeed, in one sense, the reality of an afterlife is a direct corollary of the Field view, in that the physical Field that we are will keep on manifesting as sentient minds after (what we usually consider) our own mind no longer exists. Consciousness will persist, only with different dispositions, quirks, and memories.

Our clothespin intuitions will likely struggle with this claim, as such a different state of consciousness does not intuitively feel like it will be "me" — it will, after all, be a different state. Yet what we miss is that the same is true of the stream of conscious states that we usually consider "me". As author John Updike noted:

"Each day, we wake slightly altered, and the person we were yesterday is dead."[41]

In other words, our state of consciousness *always* changes, and the only difference between the future states of consciousness that we consider "our own" and "those of others" is *the degree of similarity* of the conscious states in question. Nothing more. They are all, in a very real sense, the substance of you. And in this sense, *as the Field*, you will indeed keep on being reborn as — or rather assuming the shape of — different sentient minds.[42]

Upon accepting this view, it can be easy to let the pendulum swing in the opposite direction by dismissing all one's intuitions about death, in effect believing that death is not bad and that survival does not matter. Yet that would also be a non sequitur. For death can indeed be bad and harmful in many ways, and the Field view arguably underscores just how bad death can potentially

---

[41] Quoted from Popova, 2013.

[42] Again, this is *not* reincarnation in any traditional sense, as there are no spirits, non-physical souls, or mysteriously preserved memories here. There is just physical reality manifesting as sentient minds.

be. After all, if we are able to serve positive roles by helping to address unmet needs and suffering for other sentient beings, then even a painless death for ourselves could potentially cause vast amounts of harm in counterfactual terms.[43]

As should be clear at this point, we must be careful not to draw false implications from the universal view of personal identity, and not be too quick to throw out all the tools and practices we have in place already, many of which are hard-won and indispensable. The universal view differs radically from common sense in many ways, and sure changes many things. Yet there are also many things that it does not change, such as the innate dispositions and limitations of humans. And it is essential that we factor in these realities that cannot readily be altered, so that we avoid making claims about urgent proposals that are not in fact practically possible. Deeper reflection and a closer look at reality is called for.

---

[43] See also Vinding, 2020, sec. 8.2; Ajantaival, 2021a; 2021b.

10. REALISTIC PATHS FORWARD

The previous chapters leave a lot to be wanted in terms of how one might adopt and act on the Field view in ways that are psychologically realistic and sustainably motivating. My aim in this last chapter is to briefly provide some suggestions that may be helpful in this regard.[44]

10.1 Narrow Self-Compassion in Service of Universal Compassion

An attitude that seems indispensable is one of self-compassion. Of course, on the Field view, all compassion is ultimately self-compassion, yet I would argue that we still have reason to (also) emphasize self-compassion in the typical narrow sense. Why? One reason is that, when confronted with a large world that contains vast amounts of suffering, it can be easy to drown oneself in shame-based motivations and

---
[44] I dive deeper into this topic in Vinding, forthcoming.

admonitions. This can in turn make us feel like other states of the Field are in need of help and compassion, but that we ourselves, in the narrow sense, are not, and that we should just get to work trying to help others.

But this strict and almost self-punitive approach is not consistent with universal (self-)compassion. Not only is it exclusive in that it leaves out ourselves (in the narrow sense) from our supposedly universal compassion, but it also just seems to be a starkly suboptimal and unhealthy approach to improving the world. Persistent self-shaming is unlikely to be a sustainable approach, whereas research suggests that self-compassion, in contrast, tends to aid rather than undermine our willpower and productivity.[45]

Self-compassion can be an essential tool in a difficult world, and can help provide a sense of ease and consistent alignment toward the higher compassionate purpose of helping ourselves in the broadest sense.

---

[45] McGonigal, 2012, ch. 6; Landgraf, 2013.

10.2 Ways to Internalize the Field View

One may accept the arguments presented in previous chapters and yet still mostly fall back into a narrow perspective that sees little commonality with, and shows very limited concern for, those consciousness-moments that we typically regard as others. So how, one may wonder, can we internalize the Field view in deeper and more persistent ways? The following are some mental models and practices that I have found helpful.

10.2.1 The Totality of Consciousness-Moments: Same but Different

One helpful visualization might be to picture the totality of conscious experiences as a vast, spatially distributed set of discrete consciousness-moments, one of which is your current consciousness-moment. In this set of experiential frames, we can notice that the consciousness-moments that we usually consider "our future self" have something in common with all other consciousness-moments. That is, the experiences of our (narrowly construed) "future self" and the experiences of "others" all have in common that they are different from our current experience-moment, located elsewhere in space and time, and none of them are experienced directly by our current consciousness-moment. Furthermore, the core commonality that is found across the experiential frames of (what we typically consider) our future self — i.e. their shared property of being consciousness-moments — is also shared with all other consciousness-moments.

In short, all future experience-moments — whether they be "our own" or those of "others" — are *different* from our current one, yet they are the *same* in that they all equally share the property of being an experience-moment. And the visualization exercise described above may help us better appreciate these deep commonalities between "our future self" and "others".

10.2.2 Different Minds as Manifestations of the Same Fabric

In contrast to the discrete visualization outlined above, there is also a kind of visualization that is more continuous in nature, in that it sees all beings as different parts of the same underlying continuum. In specific terms, one might visualize different beings as parts of the same flowing river, or as different waves of the same ocean. The broad picture is thus one of a single, unitary fabric — essentially the Field — that manifests as various sentient minds.[46]

10.2.3 Seeing All Beings as One Brain That Has Been Divided

Another helpful visualization may be to picture all sentient beings as a single brain that has been divided into many different parts (as a metaphor of the Field evolving into many beings). This visualization is not fundamentally different from the visualizations outlined above, but the brain metaphor is perhaps especially helpful given that many of us are used to thinking of the brain as the carrier of personal identity.

10.2.4 Focusing on the Common Feature of Consciousness

A different approach that does not involve any conceptual visualizations is to simply focus on the common feature of consciousness shared by all sentient beings. This is a more direct approach that focuses on what is arguably the core shared feature of all sentient

---
[46] For similar metaphors, see Herrán, 2018.

minds (in phenomenological terms), and which brings this shared feature to the fore.

The seeing in question is arguably a case of "easier done than said", in that the description of the process can be much less informative and less insightful than simply looking directly, and descriptions might likewise make it sound more complicated than it is. But to provide a brief instruction: the exercise is simply to focus directly on our own experience, and to rest on the fact of its consciousness per se. Resting on this aspect of our experience, we can see that it is a common feature across *all* our experiences, which in turn renders our deep commonality with other sentient beings more clear — a commonality that can otherwise be skillfully hidden by our Darwinian minds optimized for gene propagation.

10.2.5 Practices of Self-Transcendence

Similar to the introspective exercise outlined in the previous section, there is a whole range of practices that can help us to transcend — or at least to reduce the strength of — assumed notions of a narrow and closed self. By helping us to be less caught up in the narrative of a small egoic self, these practices can likewise help free us up to see a deeper commonality with other sentient beings.

Since practices of this kind have been developed over centuries, there is little need for me to reinvent the (Dharmic) wheel here. For those who are interested in these practices, I would recommend exploring practices of anatta ("no-self") meditation, dzogchen meditation, and self-inquiry meditation.

10.2.6 Preserving a Healthy Sense of Self

It is worth reiterating, as a counterbalance to some of the points made above, that many of our ordinary intuitions can still be well worth preserving even if we shift our perspective (more) toward a universal view of personal identity. Thus, even if there is ultimately no narrow self in the sense that we typically assume (i.e. no narrow self that is substantively distinct from others in a deep ontological sense), it is likely still helpful to have an ordinary narrative sense of self for purposes of planning and goal-directed action. This is not in conflict with a universal view of personal identity, even if there may be an apparent tension.

Specifically, adopting a healthy and agentic sense of self that works to improve the world does not imply the negation of a universal view of personal identity, since such an agentic self can be reconciled with, and can in some sense be nested within, the universal view. We can see ourselves both as a broad, all-encompassing self *and* — for functional and pragmatic purposes — as a compassionately driven subset of this larger self.

10.3 Toward a More Compassionate Future Guided by Self-Understanding

The universal view of personal identity that I have presented in this book is by no means original. It has been endorsed by many people throughout history, from the authors of the Upanishads to Arthur Schopenhauer, Freeman Dyson, and Daniel Kolak (author of *I Am You*).[47] This historical convergence, combined with the observation that our common-sense view of personal identity seems untenable and is apt to be increasingly challenged in our information age, suggests that it may

---

[47] Other people and texts that appear to have endorsed this view are listed at https://en.wikiquote.org/wiki/Open_individualism

be possible to move toward a future in which the universal view of personal identity is more prevalent and in which this view guides our actions to a greater extent.

My hope in writing this book has been to steer us (slightly) closer toward such a future. In the best case, we may envision a stage of societal development in which it is the norm to see other beings as different versions of ourselves, and in which we endeavor to help all beings reach their fullest potential in sophisticated and well-coordinated ways, all aimed toward the higher compassionate purpose of alleviating severe suffering. This might, of course, sound utopian and unrealistic. Yet it is worth remembering that many tiny steps in the right direction may eventually lead to transformative change. And even if such change might be unrealistic on a large scale, it seems that even a partial realization of this compassionate ideal is still worth striving for.

ACKNOWLEDGMENTS

My deepest thanks go to David Pearce for providing support and inspiration, as well as for giving helpful feedback that benefited the book greatly. I am likewise grateful to Teo Ajantaival for helpful comments that led me to add a new chapter on realistic paths forward. Finally, I want to thank Joachim, Ailin, Magnus, Joe, and Jess for their friendship and support.

BIBLIOGRAPHY

Ajantaival, T. (2021a). Positive roles of life and experience in suffering-focused ethics.
https://forum.effectivealtruism.org/posts/t3St6Fz4DmHtKfgqm/positive-roles-of-life-and-experience-in-suffering-focused

Ajantaival, T. (2021b). Minimalist axiologies and positive lives.
https://forum.effectivealtruism.org/posts/5gPubzt79QsmRJZnL/minimalist-axiologies-and-positive-lives

Althaus, D. & Gloor, L. (2016). Reducing Risks of Astronomical Suffering: A Neglected Priority.
https://longtermrisk.org/reducing-risks-of-astronomical-suffering-a-neglected-priority/

Animal Ethics (2012/2016). Speciesism.
http://www.animal-ethics.org/speciesism/

Bentham, J. (1789/2017). *An Introduction to the Principles of Morals and Legislation*. Early Modern Texts.

Boswell, J. (2009). Symphony of Science - 'We Are All Connected' (ft. Sagan, Feynman, deGrasse Tyson & Bill Nye).
https://www.youtube.com/watch?v=XGK84Poeynk

Carroll, S. (2021). The Quantum Field Theory on Which the Everyday World Supervenes.
https://arxiv.org/pdf/2101.07884.pdf

Caviola, L. et al. (2019). The Moral Standing of Animals: Towards a Psychology of Speciesism. *Journal of Personality and Social Psychology*, 116(6), pp. 1011-1029.

Dawkins, R. (2011). Richard Dawkins on vivisection: "But can they suffer?".
http://boingboing.net/2011/06/30/richard-dawkins-on-v.html

Decety, J. et al. (2013). An fMRI study of affective perspective taking in individuals with psychopathy: imagining another in pain does not evoke empathy. *Front. Hum. Neurosci*. Published online at:
http://journal.frontiersin.org/article/10.3389/fnhum.2013.00489/full

Diebels, K. & Leary, M. (2019). The psychological implications of believing that everything is one. *The Journal of Positive Psychology*, 14(4), pp. 463-473.

Flanagan, B. (2003). Are Perceptual Fields Quantum Fields? *NeuroQuantology*, 3, pp. 334-364.

Flynn, J. (2012). *Are We Getting Smarter?: Rising IQ in the Twenty-First Century*. Cambridge University Press.

Giles, J. (1993). The No-Self Theory: Hume, Buddhism, and Personal Identity. *Philosophy East and West*, 43(2), pp. 175-200.

Gloor, L. (2016). The Case for Suffering-Focused Ethics.
https://longtermrisk.org/the-case-for-suffering-focused-ethics/

Gómez-Emilsson, A. (2015). Ontological Qualia: The Future of Personal Identity.
https://qualiacomputing.com/2015/12/17/ontological-qualia-the-future-of-personal-identity/

Hahn, T. (1993/1999). *Call Me by My True Names: The Collected Poems of Thich Nhat Hanh*. Parallax Press.

Harris, S. (2010/2011). *The Moral Landscape: How Science Can Determine Human Values*. New York: Free Press.

Harris, S. (2014). *Waking Up: A Guide to Spirituality Without Religion*. New York: Simon & Schuster.

Hayworth, K. (2015). Dr. Ken Hayworth, Part 3: If we can build a brain, what is the future of I? https://www.youtube.com/watch?v=nU9D0AlSRb8

Herrán, M. (2018). Metaphors of Open Individualism. https://manuherran.com/metaphors-of-open-individualism/

Hobson, A. (2013). There are no particles, there are only fields. *American Journal of Physics*, 81, pp. 211-223.

Hood, B. (2012). *The Self Illusion: Why There is No 'You' Inside Your Head*. Constable.

Horta, O. (2022). *Making a Stand for Animals*. Routledge.

Joot, P. (2012/2015). Quantum Mechanics II: Notes and problems from UofT PHY456H1F 2012. Published online at: http://peeterjoot.com/archives/math2011/phy456.pdf

Kaufman, S. (2018). What Would Happen If Everyone Truly Believed Everything Is One? https://scottbarrykaufman.com/what-would-happen-if-everyone-truly-believed-everything-is-one/

Kolak, D. (2004). *I Am You: The Metaphysical Foundations for Global Ethics*. Springer.

Kurzweil, R. (2012/2013). *How to Create a Mind: The Secret of Human Thought Revealed*. Penguin Books.

Lancaster, T. & Blundell, S. (2014). *Quantum Field Theory for the Gifted Amateur*. Oxford University Press.

Landgraf, A. (2013). Under Pr Under Pressure : Self-Compassion as a Pr e : Self-Compassion as a Predictor of T or of Task Performance and Persistence. https://digitalcommons.unf.edu/cgi/viewcontent.cgi?article=1432&context=etd

Leighton, J. (2011). *The Battle for Compassion: Ethics in an Apathetic Universe*. Algora Pub.

Leighton, J. (2015). The Battle for Compassion - a short film by Jonathan Leighton. https://www.youtube.com/watch?v=DBiKl_v5Mls

Low, P. et al. (2012). The Cambridge Declaration on Consciousness. https://web.archive.org/web/20131109230457/http://fcmconference.org/img/CambridgeDeclarationOnConsciousness.pdf

Maharaj, N. (1973/2012). *I Am That: Talks with Sri Nisargadatta Maharaj*. Acorn Press.

Mayerfeld, J. (1999). *Suffering and Moral Responsibility*. Oxford University Press.

McGonigal, K. (2012/2013). *The Willpower Instinct: How Self-Control Works, Why It Matters, and What You Can Do to Get More of It*. Avery.

Metzinger, T. (2009). *The Ego Tunnel: The Science of the Mind and the Myth of the Self.* Basic Books.

Parfit, D. (1984/1987). *Reasons and Persons.* Oxford University Press.

Pearce, D. (1995/2007). *The Hedonistic Imperative.* Published online at:
http://www.hedweb.com/hedab.htm.

Pearce, D. (2007). The Abolitionist Project.
https://www.abolitionist.com/.

Pearce, D. (2008). The Reproductive Revolution: Selection Pressure in a Post-Darwinian World.
http://www.reproductive-revolution.com/

Pearce, D. (2009). Reprogramming Predators.
http://www.hedweb.com/abolitionist-project/reprogramming-predators.html.

Pearce, D. (2012). The Anti-Speciesist Revolution.
http://www.hedweb.com/transhumanism/antispeciesist.html

Pearce, D. (2014). Non-Materialist Physicalism: An experimentally testable conjecture by David Pearce.
https://www.physicalism.com/

Pearce, D. (2016). Compassionate Biology: How CRISPR-based "gene drives" could cheaply, rapidly and sustainably reduce suffering throughout the living world.
https://www.gene-drives.com/

Popova, M. (2013). John Updike on Writing and Death. https://www.brainpickings.org/2013/10/10/john-updike-on-writing-and-death/

Sagan, C. (1980). *Cosmos*. Random House.

Salt, H. (ed.) (1915). *Killing for Sport*. George Bell & Sons Ltd., London

Schrödinger, E. (1936/1992). *What Is life?: The Physical Aspect of the Living Cell; with Mind and Matter; & Autobiographical Sketches*. Cambridge University Press.

Sidgwick, H. (1874/1981). *The Methods of Ethics*. Hackett Pub. Co.

Slovic, P. (2007). "If I look at the mass I will never act": Psychic numbing and genocide. *Judgment and Decision Making*. 2(2), pp. 79-95.

Speciesism: The Movie. (2012). Film. Directed by Mark Devries. Mark Devries Productions.

Strawson, G. (2006). Realistic monism: Why physicalism entails panpsychism. *Journal of Consciousness Studies*, 13(10-11), pp. 3-31.

Time Magazine (1954). Science: The Fleeting Flesh. http://content.time.com/time/magazine/article/0,9171,936455,00

Tomasik, B. (2009/2014). How Many Wild Animals Are There? http://reducing-suffering.org/how-many-wild-animals-are-there/

Tomasik, B. (2011/2016). Risks of Astronomical Future Suffering. https://longtermrisk.org/risks-of-astronomical-future-suffering/

Tomasik, B. (2013a/2015). Against Wishful Thinking.
https://longtermrisk.org/against-wishful-thinking/

Tomasik, B. (2013b/2014). Applied Welfare Biology and Why Wild-Animal Advocates Should Focus on Not Spreading Nature.
https://reducing-suffering.org/applied-welfare-biology-wild-animal-advocates-focus-spreading-nature/

Tomasik, B. (2013c/2016). The Horror of Suffering.
https://reducing-suffering.org/applied-welfare-biology-wild-animal-advocates-focus-spreading-nature/

Tomasik, B. (2015a). The Importance of Wild-Animal Suffering. *Relations*, 3(2), pp. 134-148.

Tomasik, B. (2015b/2018). Reasons to Promote Suffering-Focused Ethics.
https://reducing-suffering.org/the-case-for-promoting-suffering-focused-ethics/

Tomasik, B. (2016). Preventing Extreme Suffering Has Moral Priority.
https://www.youtube.com/watch?v=RyA_eF7W02s

Urban, T. (2014). What Makes You You?
http://waitbutwhy.com/2014/12/what-makes-you-you.html

Vinding, M. (2015). *Speciesism: Why It Is Wrong and the Implications of Rejecting It.*

Vinding, M. (2020). *Suffering-Focused Ethics: Defense and Implications*. Ratio Ethica.

Vinding, M. (2022a). *Reasoned Politics*. Ratio Ethica.

Vinding, M. (2022b). Research vs. non-research work to improve the world: In defense of more research and reflection. https://magnusvinding.com/2022/05/09/in-defense-of-research/

Vinding, M. (forthcoming). *Compassionate Purpose: Personal Inspiration for a Better World.* Ratio Ethica.

Printed in Great Britain
by Amazon